Why the critics loved
Elegant and Easy Rooms

"Author Dylan Landis gives you the skinny on design: why you shouldn't choose paint from a paint chip, how the right curtains can make a ceiling look higher, what you should spend on a rug, why objects on a mantel should be of varying heights, and on and on. Tightly written and filled with whimsical illustrations, *Elegant and Easy* is a must read for do-it-yourself design mavens."

—*Newsday*

"If the choicest thing in your apartment is the rattan blinds, don't call in the wrecking ball just yet. Instead, follow these tips from Dylan Landis . . . and give your living space a face-lift."

—*Cosmopolitan*

"The secrets are short, real, and very good. . . . How to dress a dormer window, how to heighten a room with pictures, variations on an 'endless hallway'—are just a few of the myriad topics that are wonderfully easy to understand, and fast to read."

—*Victorian Homes*

"Truly helpful hints for spaces large and small."

—*The Washington Post*

"What it promises . . . this paperback delivers . . . writer Dylan Landis . . . has an inside track to the best professional advice—covering everything from problem rooms to the art of display."

—*Better Homes and Gardens Decorating Magazine*

Books by Dylan Landis

Metropolitan Home American Style
Elegant and Easy Rooms
Elegant and Easy Bedrooms
Elegant and Easy Foyers, Halls, and Stairs
Designing for Small Homes
Checklist for Your New Baby
Your Healthy Pregnancy Workbook
Your Healthy Child's Medical Workbook
Your Health & Medical Workbook

Elegant and Easy Living Rooms

100 Trade Secrets for Designing with Style

DYLAN LANDIS
Drawings by David McGrievey

A DELL TRADE PAPERBACK

A DELL TRADE PAPERBACK
Published by
Dell Publishing
a division of
Random House, Inc.
1540 Broadway
New York, New York 10036

Dell books may be purchased for business or promotional use or for special sales. For information please write to: Special Markets Department, Random House, Inc., 1540 Broadway, New York, NY 10036.

DTP and the colophon are trademarks of Random House, Inc.

Library of Congress Cataloging-in-Publication
Landis, Dylan, 1956–
Elegant and easy living rooms: 100 trade secrets for designing with style / Dylan Landis;
drawings by David McGrievey.
p. cm.
ISBN 0-440-50859-2
1. Living Rooms. 2. Interior decoration—History—20th century. I. Title.
NK2117.L5 L36 2000
747.7'5—dc21
99-045821

Printed in the United States of America

Published simultaneously in Canada

April 2000

10 9 8 7 6 5 4 3 2 1

FFG

For Jan Gottlieb

ACKNOWLEDGMENTS

The best part of writing the Elegant and Easy books was discovering, again and again, how generous designers can be with their hard-won trade secrets. Those named on these pages were also generous with their time, making it a challenge to single anyone out—but I am particularly grateful to Kim DePole, Christopher Fox, and Barbara Southerland for providing an abundance of ideas, and to Barry Goralnick, architect and friend, who taught me much about good design.

Kenneth X. Charbonneau of Benjamin Moore shared his expertise on color. Neil Janovic of Janovic/Plaza Decorating Centers fielded my questions about paint. Erica Landis and Dean Baquet, both passionate about decorating, improved the manuscript with their thorough readings. And David McGrievey gave the book charm and spirit through his drawings.

My warmest thanks, as always, go to my literary agent, Dominick Abel. And I am fortunate to have worked with two terrific editors at Dell—Mary Ellen O'Neill, who launched the Elegant and Easy series, and Kathleen Jayes, who wrapped it up.

CONTENTS

Elegant and Easy Living Rooms

100 Trade Secrets for Designing with Style

How (and Why) to Use This Book

A room for living

Makes you think of unwinding, doesn't it? A place to steep your tea, open the mail, have a sandwich, read a book.

Now call it a living room, and suddenly the place leaps to attention. You could almost take inventory with your eyes shut: a painting hung over the sofa, check. Matching side tables, check. Identical lamps, check. Twin candelabra on the mantelpiece, check.

Friends have gathered in these formulaic rooms for years with no ill effects; indeed, such settings can be so pretty that there's nothing visibly wrong. But if you also sense that your living room stands at attention, that it's not quite as inviting as other rooms that you've admired, then your decorating may need to loosen up. In magazine-editor parlance, you need to put a twist—your own personal spin—on all that tradition.

A really good living room truly invites relaxation. It reflects your passions and eccentricities, feels inviting, and functions very much like the heart of your home.

And it's not even that hard to achieve. The tips in this book—those that appeal to you, at least—can help guide your design decisions.

WHO DREAMED UP THESE DESIGN IDEAS?

Most of the 100-plus tips, inspirational ideas, and tricks of the trade on these pages come from interior designers around the country. As a fan (and a design writer), I've spent the last decade quizzing them on the details of their work.

From all those interviews come the nuggets of design advice that pack this book. Indeed, all the designers mentioned on these pages were incredibly generous with their knowledge, and just as specific. (They had to be. If a designer recommended, say, a lavender ceiling but wouldn't name-drop her favorite paint shade, out she went. Because what good is advice that you can't take to the store?)

Still, there's a caveat: Occasionally, one tip seems to contradict another. That's because designers often disagree—for every decorator who loves white walls, there's another who finds them uninspired—and what looks glamorous in some homes may feel impractical in others. In the end, it comes down to trusting your own instincts: just follow the tips that feel right for you.

THE ELEGANT AND EASY PREMISE

The Elegant and Easy approach to living room design is both forgiving and intuitive. It lets you decorate naturally and impulsively, as inspiration strikes (or as money flows in). It encourages you to trust your instincts, tune in to color, and borrow ideas from the experts. It prompts you to spend money wisely, but also to save money creatively.

That's the premise. Here's the promise:

If you try any five ideas from these pages, you will love your living room more.

It doesn't matter if your budget runs to $500 or $50,000, or if you live in an apartment or a house. Any five of these professional design "recipes," chosen from your heart and applied in any order, will make your living room more comfortable, more sensual, more polished, or more vibrant—more of anything you wish, because *your* taste and *your* instincts are the guiding star.

Here's what you won't need: grand plans, floor plans, or ex-

quisitely educated taste. (That's how professionals work, but this book wasn't written for them.)

And let's be honest—here's what you won't get: a living room so perfect, so magnificent, and so flawlessly detailed that magazine scouts knock on your door. That's because you're probably not rich, and (even more important) you're probably not a professional designer.

But you *can* give your living room an Elegant and Easy upgrade.

THE GOAL OF IMPERFECTION

Remember that a great living room is a paradox. It has to look good for company, but it has to *feel* good for you alone. So don't try to furnish this room in its Sunday best. Think, instead, of how you might dress up a beloved pair of jeans: with pearls, silk, and fabulous shoes.

It's this kind of high-contrast mix, this marriage of comfort and class, that makes a living room both beautiful and intimate. Perfection, that Sunday-best ideal, has nothing to do with it. In fact, perfection is unattainable—dull. "When rooms look perfect, they aren't," says Craig Raywood, a New York interior designer. "When there's imperfection, personality comes through."

The late and legendary decorator Sister Parish once described a good living room as "comfortable for four, comfortable for forty." If you can also make it comfortable for one—for you—this room will become both a personal haven and a magnetic gathering spot.

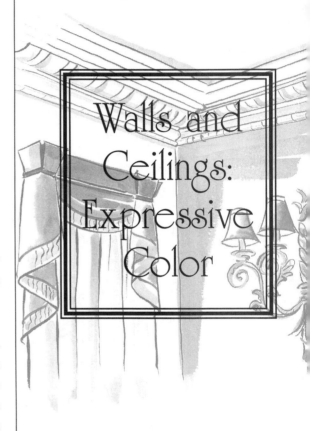

Walls and Ceilings: Expressive Color

𝓔ven people who love color—people who are drawn to yellow sweaters or scarlet silk robes—get anxious about painting their living room walls.

This is, after all, a semipublic space, and you probably learned in childhood that it's supposed to be tasteful. (Think presentable, not personal.) So if you're like most of us, you've dressed the walls and ceiling in uncontroversial white, as safely as if for a job interview.

But by playing it safe, you may be adhering to so-called rules that actually work against you. For example:

Myth No. 1: Color on the walls will make my living room look smaller.

Quite the contrary—color makes the room an unforgettable embrace. It will engage you (and your visitors) in an immediate and emotional way, even if the color is a delicate one. Color also makes you look enviably confident about your sense of style.

Here's a great guideline, applied by countless decorators: In large or sunny living rooms, lean toward lighter shades of the colors you love (for example, bay leaf green instead of hunter). In smaller or darker rooms, move toward darker or more intense color. You'll never think about the room's size or lack of sunlight again—you'll simply be taken by those gorgeous red or violet or olive-colored walls every time you walk in.

Myth No. 2: White walls will make my living room look larger.

Actually, white walls contrast so sharply with most furnishings and artwork that your living room may visually *shrink*.

If white is honestly your favorite color, you'll need more than paint to make it work. White expands a room only when it blankets the space—appearing not just on walls, but also on fabrics, furnishings, and rugs. Avoid a monochromatic space by working with a large palette, from ivory and camel to butter and pale rose. (The possibilities are rich: Janovic/Plaza Decorating Centers claims to carry 1,000 shades of off-white paint.) Add in various textures, such as leather, linen, and silk, to complete the symphony of a lavishly white living room.

A note on paint

The most practical paint is latex, not oil. It dries fast, cleans up with water, and doesn't offend the environment. Use an eggshell finish on walls, semigloss on woodwork.

Caution: Paint in rich, deep colors, particularly red, is saturated with pigment. When you wash dirt off a wall painted in eggshell latex, the red pigment may lift away, too, leaving a permanent mark.

Here are three solutions, none perfect: (1) Use eggshell latex anyway, because it looks good. Clean lightly with a sponge, which is less abrasive than cloth. (2) Use semigloss paint. It stands up well to cleaning, but you must have near-perfect walls, as the sheen highlights flaws. (3) For imperfect walls that require frequent cleaning—if you have children, say—consider oil paint.

Myth No. 3: Ceilings should always be white.

Why? Some of the prettiest ceilings around are light, atmospheric pastels: lavender, sky, delicate green. If you prefer white, at least stir a cupful of the wall color into each gallon of ceiling paint; it will subtly tie the backdrop together.

The tips that follow include actual colors that have worked for some of the top interior designers around the country. Not every color they suggest will please you—indeed, designers often disagree with each other—but at least you'll know each color has been a flaming success *somewhere,* and may be well worth trying in your own living room.

ROMANCE A SHADOWY ROOM

To brighten a living room with northern exposure, many people reflexively reach for white paint. But white walls without sunlight look drab, not bright. Instead, choose a shade of off-white that's flushed with a fresh, natural color. Magazine editor Susan Millar Perry found one of the loveliest shades I've seen: Benjamin Moore's Opal, a distinctly rose-tinted off-white. The result is a restful, romantic room that looks not sun-deprived but blessed with shade.

Tip: *To further emphasize the blush of the walls, Perry slipcovered all of her seating in white, and painted her fine-boned hearth and moldings in Benjamin Moore's Atrium White.*

THE NAIL POLISH ATTITUDE

At $10 or $15 a quart, testing a half-dozen shades of paint on the walls can constitute a $90 experiment. But for $2 apiece

plus shipping, you can purchase 4-ounce jars of more than 1,000 Pratt & Lambert colors, sampling them for less than it costs to try a new shade of nail polish. Examine paint strips at your local store, then call the Adler Brothers store in Providence, RI, to order the colors you want: (401) 421-5157.

LET THE WOODWORK REIGN

To show off terrific architecture—archways, moldings, generously framed windows—choose light or neutral colors for the walls, such as taupe, lavender, or light gray, and paint the moldings white. The subdued color will keep the room airy-looking, but they'll also set up a gentle contrast that makes the moldings pop.

A few of my favorites: New York designer Nancy Klasen's pale gray (Benjamin Moore no. 1550), Boston design firm C&J Katz's manila-folder beige (Benjamin Moore no. 141), or New York designer Debra Blair's light amethyst (Pratt & Lambert's Iris Mist, no. 1041).

A TINT OF TOBACCO

If you envision your living room as a gentleman's smoking room from an earlier, more leisurely era, try this tobacco glaze from

Christopher Fox, a Brooklyn designer. It will tinge your walls as if they had been veiled and mottled by years of cigarette smoke. Best, there's no need to apply primer first; just wash off any accumulated dust or dirt. Even dingy white walls will age handsomely.

To one gallon of acrylic glazing medium, sold at paint stores, add a drop or two (literally) of each of these four universal tints (also from paint stores, roughly $2 apiece): raw sienna, burnt sienna, raw umber, and burnt umber. Stir thoroughly. Test on an inconspicuous corner of the wall before deciding whether to add more tint. "Sienna warms a color up, umber tones it down, and a combination of the two provides the darkest 'smoke' effect," says Fox.

The technique is simple: apply to small areas with a roller or brush. Immediately "lift" some of the glaze back off with a wad of cheesecloth.

MAGNIFICENT SHADES OF WHITE

Certain hues of white, whether crisp or creamy, look good in virtually every setting. What follows is a short list of designers' favorites. Just line up the paint chips and choose. You can't go wrong.

- Bierly-Drake, a Boston design firm, favors Atrium White and no. 904, both from Benjamin Moore, and Ralph Lauren's Pocket Watch White.

- The late Mark Hampton, one of the country's premier designers, loved no. 925 and no. 932, both Benjamin Moore.

- Boston's C&J Katz swears by Benjamin Moore's White Dove.

Tip: When purchasing paint for the ceiling, avoid anything that the paint-store salesperson calls "ceiling white," which is cheaply made. Instead, paint your ceiling the same shade of white you're lavishing on the trim, says Lee Bierly of Bierly-Drake.

WHITE AND THE ART OF LAYERING

For a simple palette of whites that looks good in both natural and artificial light, designer Christopher Fox paints walls in Benjamin Moore's Navajo White—"the color of chalk, with both cool and warm tones," he says. For trim, use Ralph Lauren's Polo Mallet White.

DEEP GREENS, BRIDAL WHITES

At a prestigious designer show house in Boston, design partners Lee Bierly and Christopher Drake painted their room a deep sage green, using high-gloss paint for a light-reflecting sheen. Their room, much admired, was published in *House Beautiful*. And their secret? Benjamin Moore no. 454, a sage green that could have been lifted from an Aubusson rug.

What made it work: Bierly-Drake's use of white as the major accent color, on fabrics as well as on moldings. "A strong color on the walls doesn't have to match anything else in the room," says Bierly. "Just let it be itself, and play it against white—not just white paint, but crisp white linens, like Battenberg lace."

Tip: To use high-gloss paint, you need flawless, professionally prepared walls. The labor is costly, so consider this an investment. Bierly-Drake used oil-based enamel, but you can get fairly close with semi-gloss or high-gloss latex paint.

HOMAGE TO A RUG

It's stock decorating advice: Invest in a great rug, then key your paint colors to it. But what if you can't afford a superior rug? Consider these paint palettes adapted from antique carpets by Benjamin Moore's color marketing consultant, Kenneth X. Charbonneau.

His inspiration: fine Savonnerie carpets, originally woven for French royalty in the eighteenth century, and late-nineteenth-century Arts and Crafts rugs that draw their colors from nature. Within any one of the palettes that follow (all Benjamin Moore), you can try any combination of paints on walls, ceilings, and trim:

Savonnerie (muted): no. 1239 (chocolate), no. 1044 (ivory), no. 1205 (hushed pink), no. 1103 (camel), no. 1047 (tan).

Savonnerie (bold): no. 495 (sage), no. 052 (pale pink), no. 035 (crimson), no. 049 (reddish brown), no. 189 (ocher), no. 1053 (pale tan).

Arts and Crafts (forest): no. 440 (muted leaf green), no. 441 (forest green), no. 380 (pale green-white), no. 1295 (red berry).

Arts and Crafts (meadow): no. 386 (palest green-white), no. 531 (bay leaf), no. 388 (delicate light green), black (think night sky; use as accent color only).

COLOR WITH CHARACTER

A living room that's interrupted on every wall by windows or doorways may seem hard to decorate. In fact, it's a fine opportunity to use a strong color, because with all those doors and windows, it won't engulf you.

Among the possibilities:

- Rittenhouse Ivory, a historically accurate and warm taupe. For a brochure of paint swatches, call Old Village Paint Ltd., (610) 238-9001.

- Traditional dark red, Benjamin Moore no. 1323, favored by the late designer Mark Hampton.

- A meditative twilight violet, recommended by Bonnie Rosser Krims in her book *The Perfect Palette* (Warner Books). Krims likes Benjamin Moore no. 1419. For an even deeper violet, she suggests Benjamin Moore no. 818.

- Seedling, a medium green, or Cornmeal, an ocher yellow, both from Martha Stewart's paint line, sold at Kmart stores.

COLOR THAT CAN'T BE PINNED DOWN

Tracie Rozhon, a *New York Times* design writer who has renovated her own homes for years, always paints her living room walls in ethereal, hard-to-name colors. Being pale, these hues can make a small space feel distinctly airier. But they are just rich enough to make a room feel intimate, too. Two of Rozhon's favorites:

- Benjamin Moore no. 226. A grayed-down celery. (For display niches or built-in shelving, use the slightly darker no. 227.)

- Pratt & Lambert's Moth Gray. A pale and sophisticated mix of taupe and gray.

Tip: For doors, moldings, and ceilings, Rozhon likes Benjamin Moore's Linen White.

THE GENTLE ALLURE OF PASTELS

More atmospheric alternatives to off-white, also borrowed from *The Perfect Palette* by Bonnie Rosser Krims, are colors based on the pale green grape used for Muscadet wine. Paint the living room walls soft green (Benjamin Moore no. 491), the ceiling a faint yellow (Moore's 245). Use a slightly deeper chardonnay yellow (Moore's 270) on the walls of an adjoining room or hall.

Tip: For accents, choose fabrics or ceramics the color of red wine, advises Krims.

THE COLOR OF WARMTH

Yellow is a classic color for walls—vibrant, yet almost a neutral because it serves as a foil for many other colors. Try it in a glaze, which has marvelous depth and tonal variation, and reflects the light a bit. Here is Austin designer Hortensia Vitali's tried-and-true recipe:

Over primed walls, roll on a coat of banana yellow—Benjamin Moore HC-4 or the paler HC-5, your choice, in eggshell latex paint.

For the second coat, mix four parts Benjamin Moore Alkyd Glazing Liquid with one part Pittsburgh Paint's Ginger Brown in flat oil paint. Apply with a small natural sponge using a circular motion, and wipe off promptly with a soft, clean T-shirt, *not* bunched up.

To get the motion right, copy the "wipe on, wipe off" technique from the movie *The Karate Kid*.

Tip: For trim, try Benjamin Moore's Spanish White.

Walls and Ceilings: Expressive Color

17

INSTANT ITALY

No patience for glazing? Paint walls with Benjamin Moore no. 113, suggests designer Barbara Southerland. She calls this shade of yellow "the color of Italy."

Tip: Use Benjamin Moore no. 116,
a lighter hue, in an adjacent hall or study.

❧

WISDOM FOR WALLBOARD

Add some texture to Sheetrock walls by brushing, not rolling, the last coat of paint onto your walls. "It leaves behind slight markings, so the wall looks rubbed and beautiful," says designer Christopher Fox. His advice: Use a good sable or badger brush. Brush four strokes vertically, blend horizontally, and move onto the next spot.

THE COLOR OF PEACE

Gray-green can be mysteriously murky—a color that's hard to pin down, but very serene to live with. New York designer Laura

Bohn, known for her serene interiors painted in this color family, reveals her favorite shades, all from Pittsburgh Paint:

- Aluminum: A light gray-green that looks greener in sunlight and tends to look different as daylight changes.

- Metallic: A shade darker than Aluminum.

- Old Silver: Gray-green with an infusion of charcoal—a dark, velvety color.

Tip: Paint window frames and sills in Sherwin-Williams's Pure White, advises Bohn, to bounce sunlight into the room.

APPLY A PATINA

To gently age any wall color, apply Hortensia Vitali's gingery glaze: four parts Benjamin Moore oil-based clear glazing medium mixed with one part flat, oil-based Ginger Brown from Pittsburgh Paint.

"Ginger Brown is somewhat between a raw umber and a burnt umber, and can be used over virtually any color for a wonderful patina," Vitali says. "I've used it over light violet in a formal French living room, over light green in a garden room, even over bright coral in a little hall."

INVITE THE INFLUENCE OF LIGHT

Colors from centuries past—some surprisingly hard to name or define—can manage to be both neutral and intense at the same time. Result: a room with strong personality but peaceful character. Washington, DC, designer Barry Dixon has used these historic colors (which Benjamin Moore researched and created for the Bicentennial) with much success:

- HC-14, green with a slight golden cast.

- HC-15, a lighter green with the same undertone of gold.

- HC-19, brown leaning toward taupe.

- HC-85, a deep grayish brown.

"All of Benjamin Moore's HC colors are seasonless—earthy and cool in summer, enveloping in winter," says Dixon. "They also shift as light changes through the day, which keeps them interesting."

ONE SHOT OF COLOR

Take full advantage of niches, however deep or shallow they may be. Upholster the walls in fabric (try Indian spreads, using their borders to frame the walls of the niche). Paint the niche in a magnetic color, like lavender, green, or red. Hang one fabulous painting there, or shelve the recessed space with glass (for collectibles) or wood (for books).

DEVISE A COLONNADE

Wallpaper need not cover the entire wall: trompe l'oeil wallpaper columns, for example, can march around the living room like a colonnade. They also make glamorous room dividers, says Ron Becker, a Washington, DC, designer. In an L-shaped living room, apply one column on each side of the opening to the dining area, or run three columns along each wall of the ell.

Resource: Wallpaper columns by Gramercy are 13 inches wide and come in three pieces—column, base, and capital—so you can determine the height. For retailers or other information, call (800) 988-7775.

Tip: A dark or richly colored wall, used as background, gives the paper columns more depth.

WARM UP A COOL CEILING

A cathedral ceiling, left white, can appear more looming than liberating—making a living room feel oversized and remote. Chicago designer Richar paints these lofty ceilings a light, atmospheric color, which tethers them to a more human scale while evoking the sky. His favorite shades: sage green, pale gray, airy blue.

Richar custom-mixes his own paint. The recommendations for "sky ceilings" that follow are my own, from the Donald Kaufman Color Collection, a line with unusual depth and complexity of color:

Pale green: DKC 11, a slightly watery hue, as if distilled from mist.

Pale blue: DKC 37, part cloud, part sky, very delicate.

Pale gray: DKC 8, a soft, feathery gray.

> *Tip:* These pigment-rich paints can be ordered by mail. There is a charge for DKC swatches because of their unusual size (4 by 8 inches). For information, call Donald Kaufman Color at (800) 977-9198.

THE TAUPE CEILING

New York designer Marshall Watson has created a paint palette for too-high ceilings: he paints walls in Benjamin Moore no. 170 (yellow), moldings in Moore's White Dove, and the ceiling in Moore's HC-81 (a historically correct shade of taupe). The room, he promises, will warm right up.

Walls and Ceilings: Expressive Color

THE GLORIOUSLY LOFTY CEILING

Boost low ceilings by applying crown molding—specifically, says Watson, Orac Decor's Avalon cornice molding, no. C332 (from the catalog Outwater Plastics, listed in Chapter 6, and other home-design outlets). This crown molding covers more ceiling than wall, which has the effect of making the walls seem taller. (Note: This is not a do-it-yourself job.)

Paint the molding and ceiling with Benjamin Moore's Dove

White, Watson suggests. Make the wall color at least slightly darker in tone.

Tip: To add even more "height," have your contractor buy
a simple slender molding and make a square on the ceiling
that's set 12 inches in from the Orac Decor. Paint this molding with
Dove White, too. Now, for the 12 inches of ceiling that are
between the two moldings, apply a paint mix that's half
Dove White, half of your chosen wall color.
Your ceiling will surge even higher.

EVOKE THE SKY

Consider a light blue ceiling over white walls, regardless of the height of the room. Not only is it a hint of sky, but as the traditional color for porch ceilings, it really brings the outside in.

A few to try, all Benjamin Moore, from color marketing consultant Ken Charbonneau: no. 765 (sky blue), no. 757 (robin's egg blue), or no. 660 (light blue tinged with green).

CREATE HEIGHT WITH PAINT

To boost a low ceiling, designer Marshall Watson often relies on color contrasts. His formula:

Paint the walls darker than the ceiling (use any two colors, or shades of a color, that you wish). Then, using the darker wall color, paint a 6-inch-wide border all the way around the edge of the ceiling, as if framing it. The central, lighter area of the ceiling will now look higher.

To magnify the effect, leave 6 inches of white space between the edges of the ceiling and your darker painted frame. The central framed area, now smaller, will look even higher.

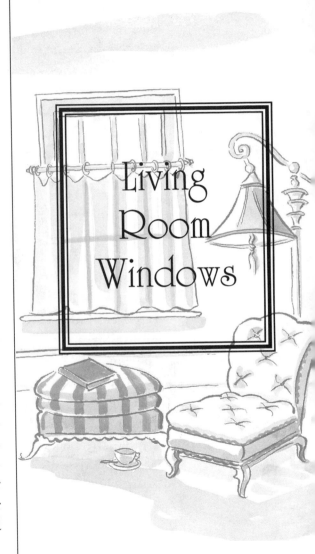

Living
Room
Windows

A good curtain is like a favorite dress. It drapes handsomely, looks well made even if it's Shaker-simple, tempts you to touch the fabric, and suits the window it was made for.

But it is definitely not your mother's drapery. *Your* curtain can hang from plumbing pipe or a birch branch instead of a rod. Its panels can be asymmetrical —one long, one short. (Or one purple, one pink.) It can hang behind a sheer instead of in front. And the sheer needn't even be white: try copper-colored sheers, if you feel bold, or chocolate-colored velvet with a burned-in, translucent pattern of swirls.

How do you decide what your windows should wear? Consider the advice of Chicago designer Richar, who can walk into a living room and swiftly gauge if the window dressing should be lavish, tailored, or barely there. "If the room has a lot going for it—great art, furniture, or architecture—you should simplify the window treatments," he says. "If the room is not that outstanding, go ahead and really decorate the window."

Alternatively, let the view guide you. If it's riveting, keep the draperies or blinds neutral in color and subdued in style so the view dominates. If it's indifferent, let the curtains reign.

Remember that dressing your living room windows is a little like getting dressed up yourself for the theater: finery isn't required, but a certain attention must be paid to style, quality, and tailoring. You can do without frills and formality, which in the language of curtains means swags, jabots, and voluptuous valances. But good fabrics, and good construction, are essential.

Unless you are truly the master of your sewing machine, have your window treatments professionally made. A tailor can do simple stitchery, if need be, but for anything involving linings or dressmaker details, ask a fabric or home-design store to recommend a drapery workroom.

THE TRANSLUCENT SOLUTION

Unlike the filmy white veils always seen in bedrooms, sheer draperies in the living room can lean toward the exotic or substantial. Invest in something with texture or color: a puckered, bubbly synthetic, a sheer bronze metallic fabric, or a translucent burgundy silk. No dressmaker details required: have the sheers hemmed with chain weights (a string of tiny metal beads), and hang as simply as possible.

Tip: Sheers, because they lack a protective opaque lining, can have a slow but ultimately fatal reaction to sun.
Your sheers may need replacing in a couple of years, especially if you face south.

UPDATE THE CAFÉ CURTAIN

Café curtains, which traditionally cover the lower half or bottom third of a window, offer privacy while admitting light from the top. To make them look fresh and elegant, says Richar, modernize the proportions. Instead of hanging the curtains halfway up the window, he raises them one mullion higher. (Mullions are the wooden strips between panes of glass.) In a window without mullions, raise the curtain roughly a foot above

the halfway point; experiment until the proportions look right. Consider curtains of white linen with a simple pinch pleat, using pinch-pleat hardware from any fabric shop.

Tip: Align your curtain rod with the mullions, cautions Richar, or the window treatment will look disorganized.

REVEAL THE GLASS

Draperies, when parted, should not cover the sides of the window itself—they should pull back farther and cover the wall alongside it. That way the window itself looks bigger and you won't block the light or view. New York designer Marshall Watson allows draperies to overlap the sides of the window by only 3 inches, and he extends them an extra 12 inches onto the wall on each side. (Your rod, therefore, must be 24 inches longer than the width of the window and trim combined.) "This opens up the window tremendously," Watson says.

RAISE HIGH THE CURTAIN ROD

Start curtains as close to the ceiling or crown molding as possible, and make sure they kiss the floor, as designers delicately

put it. Your windows and your ceiling will both appear taller. (This works best when you allow for shrinkage—wash or dry-clean the fabric *before* curtains are made.)

Tip: The same principle applies to valances that run across the tops of windows: hang them high, so they cover the wood trim without obscuring the sky.

THE LUXURY OF LINEN

If you live in a hot climate or are blessed with southern exposure, consider the simplest drapery in the world, used by New Orleans designers Ann Holden and Ann Dupuy. Though Holden and Dupuy do some of the priciest interiors in the South, they usually hang plain, unlined swaths of inexpensive linen at the windows. Yes, the linen rumples. (Let it.) Yes, it eventually yellows in the sun, and must be replaced. But it has an easy elegance.

Hang the linen from a dark-stained wooden pole using wooden rings (from any fabric shop) that you sew to the top of the draperies.

Tip: Wash the curtain and let dry in the sun before hemming. Do not iron.

THE SHEEREST SHADE

For a sophisticated sheer that is worthy of the living room, Marshall Watson devised a treatment that is half curtain, half shade.

Hem (at top and bottom) a flat panel of sheer fabric—wool, linen, even a sheer metallic—so it precisely covers the window like a banner. Slip a brass curtain rod through both hems, letting the ends of the rod extend an inch past the shade on either side. Hang the top rod from hooks on the wood trim so the sheer drapes before the window like a delicate flag.

To raise the shade, you'll need to install a pair of cup hooks or plant hooks, one on each side of the window, as high as you can comfortably reach. Lift the bottom rod and set it in the hooks.

The top of the window will still be veiled by the sheer; the bottom reveals a partial view and can now admit the breeze.

SPOTLIGHT THE DRAPERIES

To underscore a gorgeous window treatment, Watson installs downlights in the ceiling—a bigger project (involving electrical work and, sometimes, plastering) than you may desire. The low-budget version? Plant an uplight, available at any lighting store, at the foot of the draperies, concealing the fixture behind a piece of furniture. This looks especially good with sheers, Watson says,

though be aware that outsiders can see through lighted sheers at night. (Translation: Restrict this effect to the living room.)

Tip: Buy an incandescent uplight. Halogen bulbs can be a fire hazard if placed near fabric or furnishings.

THE ARTFULLY BARE FANLIGHT

How do you cover fanlights—those half-round, Palladian-style windows that arch above regular windows? Some people just can't leave them alone, topping them with Easter-bonnet swags or obscuring them with pleated fanlike shades.

Better to let a fanlight breathe. Hang simple blinds or draperies that cover only the main rectangular window. Or install curtains from a rod *above* the fanlight, as some designers do. Both treatments have the virtue of simplicity, always a good approach to architectural ornament.

THE SENSUAL SHUTTER

Sheers in the living room require a little architecture. Hang yours from a pair of hinged elbow rods, which allow you to swing the sheers like shutters away from the window. Or do

away with the flutter entirely: stretch the sheer panels taut between two elbow rods, top and bottom, so that they truly function as shutters—a polished treatment (and a signature of New York designer Mariette Himes Gomez). Both versions give you the softness of fabric without fuss.

Tip: To increase privacy, gather the "shutter" fabric on the elbow rods.

ONE MAGNIFICENT HEM

Good construction, all by itself, can make a simple drapery look expensive. Austin designer Hortensia Vitali makes plain, unpatterned curtains in a neutral color—but when she gives them an 18-inch weighted hem, a quiet grandeur emerges. (Ask for beaded-chain weights when the curtains are made.) Have the drapery lined and interlined. "It looks rich and heavy," Vitali says, "and it makes the sound in the room very peaceful and soft."

Tip: Hang the draperies high so you get the full effect of fabric sluicing down to an aristocratic hem.

RESTORE A SENSE OF BALANCE

If windows are set asymmetrically into the wall, you can rebalance the room by curtaining the entire wall from ceiling to floor, then opening the draperies just enough to reveal the windows. Instead of noting the imbalance, says Nan Lee, a partner in the New York architecture and design firm Lee/Wimpenny, your eye will take in the entire curtain and will presume symmetry where none exists.

THE ALWAYS SOPHISTICATED STRIPE

At the Harlem United Show House in New York, designer Roderick N. Shade hung elegant, broadly striped curtains that gave his room a costly custom look—yet are simple to adapt. To stripe each curtain panel, he sewed together three lengths of fabric: one in camel, one in cream, one in olive green. (The cream fabric reappeared elsewhere in the room as a slipcover, which settled harmony over the entire space.) The designer's tips:

- Choose three colors of similar intensity. Low contrast, as with Shade's three neutral colors, makes a room more serene.

- Use only one type of fabric. Shade chose a linen-cotton blend, crisper than plain cotton.

Living Room Windows

37

- For each color, cut the 54-inch-wide yardage (an industry standard) in half the long way. Have a drapery workshop sew three strips together, with a basic curtain lining, to make each curtain panel. Remember, when arranging colors, that your left and right panels must be mirror opposites.

- Repeat all three colors on throw cushions—a detail that adds polish.

BEJEWEL THE DRAPERY

We pin ornaments on our clothes—why not on our curtains? Try this: Take the lower part of the curtain's leading edge (that is, the inside edge), lift it up and diagonally across toward the outside edge, and affix with a favorite pin. Your curtains can wear pins anywhere that strikes your fancy: near the hem, along an edge, or up and to the side (about where you'd site it on a sweater, proportionally) or on the tiebacks.

Source: In addition to your own costume or silver jewelry, try the curtain jewelry—little gold stars, buttons, fleurs-de-lis, and other ornaments—from the Country Curtains catalog (see Chapter 6).

BEJEWEL THE DRAPERY II

The Elizabethans sewed gems to their draperies—a luxury that inspired designer Wilbert Louis Shaw at the Harlem United Show House in New York. For his room, Shaw stitched chandelier crystals along the top, bottom, and leading (or inside) edge of his sheer curtains. Chandelier crystals, easily found for about $1 apiece at flea markets, already have a convenient hole at the top, and not only enhance sunlight but can create a sparkle in light-deprived rooms as well.

BEJEWEL THE DRAPERY III

This variation on the crystal-bedecked curtains, from Brooklyn designer Christopher Fox, creates a drapery that is part sheer, part opaque, and worthy of a royal harem.

Cut a plain store-bought curtain into two pieces: a short top (6 or 9 inches long, not counting the rod pocket or tabs) and a long bottom. Between them, stitch a panel—8 to 12 inches high and as wide as the rest of the curtain—of sheer voile.

Sew crystals just along the top seam, where voile meets curtain fabric. The sheer quality of the voile and the diamondlike glint of the crystals make a positively sensuous marriage.

CURTAIN COUTURE ON CONSIGNMENT

A handful of cities have stores like The Curtain Exchange in
New Orleans, where custom draperies and fabric shades,
originally made for designers' clients (who later move or re-

decorate) or for show houses, are sold on consignment. Often you can get superb tailoring and detailing for one-third the cost of new work. (New curtains are also in stock, designed by the owners.) Happily, the New Orleans service works by mail: if you send photos of your living room windows, along with window measurements, a style request (modern, Victorian, etc.), and any relevant paint chips, fabric swatches, or photos, the Curtain Exchange will send you Polaroids of curtains or shades—which you may later try out on approval.

For more information, contact The Curtain Exchange, 3947 Magazine Street, New Orleans, LA 70115; tel. (504) 897-2444.

CURTAIN COUTURE BY MAIL

If you read the major design magazines, you've probably seen the drapery ads for The Silk Trading Co. They offer just a handful of styles, but all of their curtains, custom-made and mail-ordered, have a couture look that's worthy of any living room. They also make matching paints. For a catalog, contact The Silk Trading Co., 360 South La Brea, Los Angeles, CA 90036; tel. (213) 954-9280, or www.silktrading.com.

ERECT A TRANSLUCENT WALL

Not every curtain hangs before a window. Some are portieres, hanging in doorways; others are room dividers—like this one, a modern drapery devised by New York designer Craig Raywood to divide a dining ell from the rest of his living room:

Choose a curtain rod of substance and thickness. To figure its length, measure the opening of the ell: the curtain, extending from one wall, should cover less than half—but more than one-third—of the opening. Mount it to the ceiling so it extends from one end of the opening, using standard mounting hardware from fabric and home-decor shops.

Make the drapery, in contrast to the rod, just a breath of material: Raywood used two layers of sheer white chiffon, sewn together along the top and edged in white grosgrain ribbon. The chiffon's sheer delicacy makes it a breathtakingly simple room divider, like a translucent wall.

Tip: *To heighten the elegance,*
order the curtain rod in brass instead of wood.

MODERATE THE SUN

Southern exposure can make a room radiant—while fading the fabrics, pictures, and furnishings. To block some of glare, heat, and ultraviolet rays without vanquishing the view, consider mesh shades. You've probably seen them in offices: white shades perforated with thousands of pin-size holes, through which you see the view as if through a veil. These shades, by various manufacturers, can be ordered through most window-treatment suppliers, including the Smith+Noble Windoware catalog (see Chapter 6).

Two buying tips from Janovic/Plaza Decorating Centers: Spend a little more money for the chain-operated shades, which hold up better. And choose an "openness factor" of 10 percent; it offers a good compromise between how much you can see out and how much the neighbors can see in.

MODERATE THE SUN II

If your tastes run to the minimalist and the modern, try Solar Screen shades made of Mylar—the translucent film that hangs in store windows and protects the merchandise from sun. Mylar shades can hang behind drapery, but used alone, they offer a stark, edgy look (especially against white walls) while cutting down on heat, glare, and ultraviolet rays. The best color for residential use, says Janovic design consultant Franco Galvano, is Smoke/Smoke, a deep but still translucent hue.

Living Room Windows

The Glorious Sofa (and Other Seductive Seating)

𝒜 good sofa is one you can't resist. It beckons when you pass, inviting you to actually enjoy your own living room between dinner parties. To achieve this degree of bonding, you may have to replace your present sofa, a process not unlike buying a new car: quality, comfort, and seductiveness are key factors, and yes, they are expensive.

Don't buy a sofa with your in-laws and guests in mind. Buy it for *you*. See if it seduces—does it tempt you to stretch out lengthwise with a magazine, or prompt you to sit up straight? Trust the sigh that escapes when you sit down for a test drive. It indicates generosity of scale, some percentage of goosedown filling, and the kind of quality you can spot from across the room.

Perhaps you already own a good sofa (or love seat, or armchair)—"good" meaning it has a handsome shape, a solid frame that doesn't creak, and a high aaaah factor. New upholstery or a slipcover may be all you need, especially with a well-built vintage sofa that was built to last forever. Remember, though, that good upholstery is artisan's work, and priced accordingly. When a designer in a magazine crows that her curvaceous vintage love seat cost only $449, she's not mentioning the $2,000 to $3,000 she spent resuscitating it (the cost of 10 yards of mohair, new goosedown, and labor).

If your old sofa doesn't merit saving, donate it to charity and shop for seating—antique, vintage, or new—that feels truly inviting. Don't rush: any piece you buy just to fill a gap will prove an expensive albatross.

When shopping, you may face the sofa–versus–love-seat dilemma. Love seats are viable alternatives to the sofa; indeed, some designers prefer them because sofas rarely seat three people anyway—no one wants to get stuck in the middle. On the other hand, sofas are classics, and let you stretch out to read. Either way, you truly can't make a mistake if you buy what you love.

Finally, if you're budgeting, cut corners as creatively as you like—but not here. Upholstered furniture is a worthy investment.

THE SERENE SOFA

Patterned fabric can be beautiful, but it may not be the wisest choice for seating. Choose a solid color, advises New York designer Benjamin Noriega-Ortiz. That way, you won't force everything else in the room to conform to a large, patterned sofa. For throw pillows, make your own, using the same color but in different materials to create an orchestra of textures. "A room filled with furnishings," explains Noriega-Ortiz, "constitutes a pattern all by itself."

Tip: If you're drawn to this vision of simplicity but can't resist a beautiful print, save it for throw pillows.

THE ART OF CONTRAST

Before choosing a sofa color, decide what you're trying to show off. To draw attention to artwork, upholster (or slipcover) the sofa in a solid color that approximates the wall color. Your eye

will go straight to the one thing that doesn't match—the artwork, says Austin designer Hortensia Vitali.

Conversely, if the sofa is a deserving antique, upholster it to contrast with the wall color. It will demand immediate attention.

HOW TO BUY A CLASSIC

Choose a sofa, not a love seat, advises Washington, DC, designer Barry Dixon. Two people can share it without being squashed together, and a sofa is also friendlier for one person lounging lengthwise. Dixon's shopping tips follow:

- Buy a sofa in beige linen or a similar material. "It's fresh, but still basic," the designer says, and with a neutral color it's hard to make mistakes.

- Choose a simple, clean-lined style that isn't tied to any period of time, won't call undue attention to itself, and will be easy to slipcover later on.

- Look for (or custom-order) a sofa with a single long seat cushion. "Two cushions suggests a glorified love seat, and three looks choppy," says Dixon. "But one cushion looks like a classic."

A MARRIAGE OF SOFAS

If you entertain often (or live with someone who likes lounging on the sofa as much as you do), buy a matched pair of 6-foot-long sofas. Set them perpendicular to the fireplace, facing each other. Place a coffee table 48 inches square or larger between them, says Barbara Southerland, a designer based in Greenville, NC, and New York. Add a pair of chairs opposite the fireplace, and you've achieved something many people struggle with for years: a congenial arrangement in which none of the furniture is backed up stiffly against the wall. As long as your living room has the space for two sofas, says Southerland, "It's a foolproof arrangement."

UNMOOR THE SOFA

Most homeowners back their sofas up to the wall as if observing a decorating law—but most *designers* float sofas away from the wall to make the room feel more expansive. A few rules create balance and order:

- Place the sofa so it's not greeting guests with its back. A shapely love seat may offer a nice rear view, but a long sofa should be first glimpsed from the front or the side.

- Leave at least 3 feet between furnishings for major traffic arteries (the routes people take through the room).

- For smaller routes, or the little paths you follow in choosing a seat, leave 2 feet. This avoids squeezing, but keeps chairs neighborly.

EMPLOY A SOFA TABLE

If, in the end, you back the sofa up to the wall, create depth by sliding a sofa table behind it. Long, skinny, and about as tall as the sofa back, this table takes up little space while offering a

surface for lighting, books, flowers, magazines. The sense of dimension that results is particularly effective in a small room.

CONTROL THE SOFA'S SPRAWL

If your living room runs small, remember that one fabulous and overscaled piece of furniture, like a luxurious sofa, can trick the eye into perceiving a larger space. But be wary of sofas with very broad rolled arms. "Wide arms can cost you a foot of space on each side," says Nan Lee of New York's Lee/Wimpenny Architecture and Interior Design. Instead, choose a sofa with moderate or narrow arms that leave room for a side table, making the room more functional.

FURNISH ONLY FOR YOURSELF

Avoid the error that New York designer Carl D'Aquino most often sees: the living room overcrowded with seating for parties. "Don't furnish for the fourteen people you sometimes have over," he advises. "Furnish it for your own family—then bring in the dining chairs when you have a large gathering. It makes life so much easier."

You'll need comfortable and classic dining chairs, of course. D'Aquino's favorite: black oval-backed chairs upholstered in white fabric. "They're agreeable with any decor," he says.

INVEST IN DEEP COMFORT

When you slipcover or reupholster your sofa, have new seat cushions made with goosedown inside. You don't even need to splurge on 100 percent goosedown. "It lets you sink too deeply into the sofa, and it always needs refluffing," says Amy Crain, president of the catalog Room (see Chapter 6). Instead, ask for goosedown with a foam core. This combination is softer and longer-lasting than foam alone, yet more resilient (and cheaper) than pure goosedown.

MIX CHAIRS LIKE COMPANY

Let your armchairs be generous in spirit and scale. (Think of them as mini-sofas and you'll get the idea.) Collect chairs that are largely mismatched, so they won't look department-store new. Look for curves in the back or arms, as curves have a more come-hither look than angular lines; have seat cushions stuffed with down around a foam core. Finally, buy an ottoman, or have your upholsterer make one. It turns any armchair into an instant chaise longue, and doubles as extra seating.

Tip: Unless you like a historical look,
allow no more than one wing chair in your living room.
The traditional wing chair is a bit too upright for comfort.

❧❧❧

The Glorious Sofa (and Other Seductive Seating)

55

THE DANCE OF PATTERNS

If your living room feels too staid, try giving one armchair some intrigue by recovering it with two different fabrics—one for the seat cushion, and a second for the rest of the chair. (Or one for the back and outside of the chair, one for the interior and seat.)

To make this marriage of fabrics pleasing, keep the two materials closely related. Imagine ivory damask paired with ivory stripes, a zebra print against solid black, or a blue and yellow Provençal print paired with solid blue. Aim for contrast, not clash.

GIVE YOURSELF A READING NOOK

Every living room deserves one deeply comfortable reading chair. "When the house gets chaotic," says Barbara Southerland, "that chair makes your living room a perfect retreat for one." For this chair, if for no other, invest in a down-filled cushion. Add a reading lamp to the left of the chair (or, if you're left-handed, to the right, to avoid shadows on the page), and a small table for books and drinks.

THE ANGULAR ARRANGEMENT

To pry open a small or awkwardly shaped living room, turn one major piece of furniture—a sofa, love seat, or statuesque armchair—at an angle. Turn the rug at the same angle, if it's small enough. By forcing part of a rectangular room into a diagonal stance, you can make the space feel airier.

Tip: To dispel shadows in the empty corner created by an angled sofa, fill the space with a tall tree (bamboo makes an interesting break from the usual ficus) or a standing screen.

COLLECT FINE-BONED CHAIRS

Every living room needs "perching chairs," says Lee Bierly of Boston's Bierly-Drake Associates. These are the straight-backed side chairs (with no arms) that get pulled up to the coffee table in a crowd, or carried into the dining room for big dinners. When they aren't in use, back them up against the wall. Deploy them like bookends: if you have a tall bookcase or cabinet, stash a chair on either side.

Buy perching chairs for their good looks. It's hard to go wrong with classic styles:

- Thonet (bentwood) chairs, especially in black.

- Louis XVI–style chairs, noted for their delicate neoclassical lines.

The Glorious Sofa (and Other Seductive Seating)

- Molded plywood chairs from the 1950s, designed by Charles Eames.

- Antique ladder-back chairs with rush or webbed seats.

Tip: When a side chair is out of use, stand a framed print or watercolor on its seat, leaning against the back—a trick I learned from a Vicente Wolf interior.

UPGRADE THE WINDOW SEAT

Is your living room graced by a built-in window seat? Order a cushion that's a plush 3 to 4 inches thick, stuffed with goose-down around a foam core, advises New York upholsterer Jeff Alexander. Forget plain seams—adorn your cushion with contrasting welting or moss fringe. Add a couple of small throw pillows in touchable fabrics, like raw silk or chenille. Enjoy.

CONQUER AN EMPTY CORNER

What if your living room isn't fully furnished yet? Deal swiftly with a glaringly bare corner by installing a chair—any chair. Now accessorize: Add a cigarette table with flowers on it, a

floor lamp, a footstool. The corner will look hospitable until you find permanent furnishings. "It's a place to sit down and reflect," explains Hortensia Vitali. "And even if you don't use it, it establishes a human scale."

SEND A SIGNAL OF EASE

Don't rush to cover your seating in the finest fabric you can afford—it may send a don't-touch signal of formality. "Too much velvet and damask can discourage you from using your own living room," cautions Barbara Southerland. "Taupe linen, toile, cotton—these invite you to be more casual." Save the dressy fabrics you love for accents on pillows or side chairs, and you'll still get a feeling of luxe.

VEIL AN ELEGANT CHAIR

For a note of romance that affects an entire living room, Benjamin Noriega-Ortiz likes to slipcover one well-shaped side chair in translucent white fabric. It looks both virginal and sculptural, he says, and diffuses the shape of the chair. Choose a chair with a lovely silhouette (and no pattern on the upholstery), and have the slipcover professionally made of sheer white silk. "Remember that you're making a *dress* for

the chair," advises Noriega-Ortiz. "The simpler the slipcover, the nicer it looks: not too many pleats or seams."

Tip: To get the gauziest possible look, ask the slipcover-maker to roll the hems.

❦

COURT AN UNUSUAL CHAIR

Next time you swoon over a quirky chair at a flea market, snap it up. "Every living room needs one odd chair for punch," says Southerland. This might be a corner chair, a Windsor chair, or a vintage Lloyd Loom wicker chair painted Charleston green—something with personality that refuses to match anything else in the room. Follow your own taste, urges Southerland, but bear in mind one rule: The "odd chair" works best if it shows some age.

ENGAGE THE FLOOR

Rediscover the floor cushion—not to evoke your dormitory days but to invite the kind of languorous lounging once associated with opium dens. For her home furnishings catalog, Room, Amy Crain created a floor cushion that's *5 feet square—*

that is to say, irresistibly enormous—and 12 inches thick, covered with alpaca.

You can have a similar pillow made by your own upholsterer. (Crain stuffed hers with merino wool, but if you're making your own, she recommends a down-and-feather mix around a foam core.) Make the removable cover of some lush fabric, such as ultrasuede, velvet, or brocade. Toss on a couple of luxurious-looking throw pillows. Sprawl.

Living
Room
Furniture in
Supporting
Roles

They may not look like key players, but the pieces in orbit around your sofa—the tables, desks, lamps, cabinets, bookshelves, and rugs—can telegraph subtle messages about your personal style. They're also cues to you, and your guests, about how much relaxation the room "allows."

Matching side tables, for example, make one sit up a little straighter. So does a coffee table that's too far away, making you work for the privilege of setting down your drink. And so does a roomful of furniture that's stylistically safe—a quality that emerges when things feel too new, too predictable, or too proper in their symmetry.

On the other hand, imagine a living room in which every chair has a table within easy reach. The coffee table has a story to tell—perhaps it's a salvaged stained-glass window on a wrought-iron base, or not a table at all but a pair of hand-carved African stools. Perhaps the shelves are built in, creating a sense of architectural conviction, or the rug is turned at a slant, giving the room new dimension.

Even if this second room is full of flaws, it engages your eye right away. It also breaks a few rules, which sends a subliminal signal that it's okay to relax.

Try, then, to make at least one unorthodox or unexpected decision with your ancillary furnishings. Dream up a coffee table that surprises and delights you. Embrace antiques: just two pieces with patina will hint at the past, and imply that you're collecting good things over time. Make room for a vintage cabinet, a strikingly modern table, or a beautiful writing desk. It's the old and the unusual that take the starch out of a room—and make it a magnetic gathering spot.

CREATE A GRACIOUS WORKSPACE

Boston designers Lee Bierly and Christopher Drake always plant a desk in their clients' living rooms, because it makes the space doubly useful. Sometimes the desk is an antique secretary with glass-enclosed shelves that serves for both writing and storage. More often, they place a classic writing desk behind the sofa (like a console) or beside it (to double as a side table).

A desk in the living room is about display, not just work. Your pens, and the container that holds them, should be a pleasure to look at. A lacquered tray or box can marshal the papers you're working on. And the lamp should give you visual enjoyment as well as light.

THE SOCIABLE BAR

Hunt down an antique cabinet that can function as a bar, Bierly and Drake suggest. Even if it holds only two bottles of wine, a corkscrew, and a few vintage glasses, a bar is an excuse to lure friends into a room you might otherwise save for formal occasions. Art deco storage units, glass-doored bamboo cabinets, even contemporary pieces can serve as a pared-down bar, and let you store or display other objects as well.

THROW AN ALLURING CURVE

If your sofa and chairs tend to be linear and modern, install a few supporting-role furnishings with curves. The contrast only heightens a modernist look, and just as critical, it conveys a sense of comfort. Curves can appear almost anywhere: in table-tops and legs, ceramic ginger-jar lamps, the broken pediment (a classical architectural detail) above an antique secretary desk. Indeed, if the curve radiates strength—like a round contemporary rug—the room may need only one.

AN INDOOR GARDEN, TERRACED

Library steps, whether antique or reproduction, offer a graceful way of amassing small plants that might otherwise dot the room like stragglers. Make sure the piece you purchase has at least three steps; place it near the window, and set pots on every step. Create a mix in which some plants spike up while others drip over. Edit the grouping so that none of the plants looks bedraggled, and none of the pots is plastic. Aim for mass and height, setting the tallest plants on the top step.

DESIGN AROUND THE TELEVISION

If television watching is a social activity in your household, how do you integrate a TV into the living room?

Don't buy an entertainment center—it's a dead giveaway, says Barry Dixon, a Washington, DC, designer. Instead, buy an antique, vintage, or ultramodern cabinet that looks as if it could hold a bar. Hang a mirror above it; place a tray with handsome glassware on the top. Inside, where everyone will expect to see bottles, stash the TV. (Cut out the back of the cabinet if necessary.)

DESIGN AROUND THE TELEVISION II

If you can't hide the TV, Dixon advises, flaunt it. Place it on a wheeled cart—not one that trumpets "TV cart" but, rather, a vintage serving cart, a bar cart, or a sleek low table on casters. Stash videocasettes out of sight, and place books or a tray of decanters on the cart's lower shelf. "The wheels alone give the TV license to be there, because subconsciously you know it could be wheeled out of sight at any moment," says Dixon.

Tip: A small TV with a built-in VCR is most easily assimilated into a living room.

DESIGN AROUND THE TELEVISION III

Another graceful TV solution comes from designer Barbara Southerland of Greenville, NC, and New York: Build in a wall of custom bookshelves, allowing space for a 13-inch television (or TV-VCR combination) in the middle bay of shelves. "When it's surrounded by books," she says, "the TV just fades away."

Tip: Remember to coordinate the carpenter, electrician, and cable TV people so that outlets are available within the bookshelves and all cords can be hidden.

Living Room Furniture in Supporting Roles

REINVENT THE COFFEE TABLE

Anything that takes up as much floor space as a coffee table should pay you back by looking great. If it doesn't, consider replacing it with any of the following:

- An ottoman, round or square. Looks softer than wood or glass; doubles as extra seating. A tray is required for drinks or food. If you decide on a large, square ottoman, choose one with visible legs so it won't look bulky.

- A tea table or center table, 26 to 28 inches high. A vintage or antique table should retain some value over time, while a contemporary coffee table loses most of its worth the moment it leaves the store.

- Two Moroccan tables (try an import store, or the Garnet Hill catalog, listed in Chapter 6). These little tables have an exotic Moorish shape; they're also easily moved, an advantage for sofa beds.

- A low table on wheels. "Just the feeling that you could move it—even if you don't—makes a small living room feel more spacious," says Barry Dixon.

IMPLY SPACE WITH GRACE

You probably know that a glass-topped coffee table, because of its transparency, can visually enlarge a small room. Martha Stewart went a step further in her East Hampton home: she bought a glass-topped *garden* table, whose lacy iron base bore more than a hint of the spacious outdoors. Vintage garden pieces turn up at flea markets and garage sales; look for one of coffee-table height, advises Stewart, and paint it white.

Tip: For a great visual sourcebook, look at Stewart's paperback Decorating Details (*Clarkson Potter*).

THE TWO-TIERED TABLE

An oversize coffee table will appear less so if you set a small Asian altar-style pedestal on top of it, as New York designer Bunny Williams did recently at the Kips Bay Boys and Girls Club Decorator Show House. The variation in heights will detract from the table's mass and give you a second tier to use for display. Small altar and tea tables sometimes appear in the Gump's catalog (see listing in Chapter 6) and are a staple in Chinese department stores (explore the nearest Chinatown).

Tip: Books can be just as gainfully employed.
As Elizabeth Gaynor and Kari Haavisto suggest in
Stylish Solutions (Clarkson Potter),
use stacks of coffee-table books "as little pedestals to
vary the heights of the objects you display."

THE ARTFUL TABLE

Rescue a boring coffee table for less than the cost of a new one, suggests Nan Lee of the New York firm Lee/Wimpenny Architecture and Interior Design. She orders a piece of glass (from a glass supplier; check the Yellow Pages) cut to the size of

the tabletop, sets it down over a piece of antique kimono or Japanese wrapping paper, and has a carpenter frame the entire tabletop with pieces of stock molding. The frame not only holds the glass in place but makes the table look important.

Tip: Have the glass beveled,
and the entire table will look richer.

THE TRULY USEFUL TABLE

Every living room needs occasional tables—portable little tables that can be deployed wherever they're needed. Designer Barbara Southerland always has her eye out for these:

- Nesting tables, particularly antique. A trio that takes up minimal space.

- Wooden boxes on stands, like those the Victorians made to stash their precious hoards of tea.

- Old telephone tables, sometimes found on casters. Some cut a nice narrow figure and offer an unobtrusive shelf for magazines.

FOLDING TABLE REDUX

The rickety TV trays of our childhoods have been reborn, with elegant lines and handsomely patterned tops. If you see a particularly good design, snap up a pair; they offer an informal way of dining in the living room. Try catalogs like the Ballard Designs and Gump's (see Chapter 6).

THE ORGANIZING LEDGE

A display ledge for art can look insubstantial, unless it's designed like a piece of built-in furniture. New York designer Jeffrey Bilhuber created a simple architectural ledge that runs wall to wall, 12 inches deep; with no visible support, the ledge appears to float weightlessly. In truth, it is a hollow shelf, custom-made by a good carpenter who hides the metal supports inside and affixes them to the studs within the wall.

How high do you place this assertive ledge? In the living room, make it eye level for people in a seated position, says Bilhuber. "Higher if you're displaying pottery, lower for huge oil paintings," he adds.

GLIMPES OF LIGHT

Flashes of mirror are important in a small living room because they add both brilliance and dimension, like little windows, says Nan Lee. Instead of simply hanging mirrors, Lee integrates them with the furniture: "If you have an old cabinet or bookcase with glass-front doors," she suggests, "have a glazier replace the glass with beveled mirror." Its reflections and shine will immediately engage the eye.

Alternatively, replace a small table's glass top with a beveled mirror top. Whether bare or topped with objects, it has a kaleidoscopic sparkle.

RICH-LOOKING RUGS ON A BUDGET

"If you can't find the carpet you want," designer Mica Ertegun once told *Architectural Digest*, "go for sisal." A natural and neutral-colored carpeting, sisal comes relatively cheap (several hundred dollars can buy a rug 6 by 9 feet or larger), but it looks rich and fresh—which is why, every spring, the Victorians rolled up their beautiful rugs and unfurled the sisal.

Buy a big rug with black canvas binding, as unbound rugs can have an unfinished look. Layer a smaller Oriental rug on top, if you have one. Buy a rug with a latex backing, or use a rug pad underneath; maintain with regular vacuuming, and blot up spills immediately.

SCALE UP THE RUG

An undersize rug, unless part of a grouping, can end up with all the impact of a doormat. Karastan, the rug manufacturer, offers this advice: Imagine that you're using the rug to frame the major seating arrangement in your living room, and measure accordingly. (If in doubt, make a "rug" with the pages of your morning newspaper, expanding it until the size looks right—then measure.)

For a more opulent look, buy a rug so large that it leaves only about 2 inches of floor space showing between the rug's edge and the wall. On wooden floorboards, heighten the drama by painting a black border around the floor.

Tip: To give a small rug more drama in a large room, set one large chair at an angle, then align the rug with the chair.

Living Room Furniture in Supporting Roles

THE FANCIFUL HAMMOCK

If your living room is one of charm and whimsy—meaning it feels like a cross between a country cottage and an inviting front porch—why not break the rules and hang a hammock indoors?

Have a good carpenter or handyperson gauge the situation, so your hammock is supported by beams in the ceiling or studs in the walls. Layer your hammock with beautiful throw pillows and a luxurious throw—it's the addition of fine materials that upgrades your hammock to indoor status.

Source: Pretty hammocks sometimes turn up in the Legacy catalog (see Chapter 6).

BRIGHTEN A DECEMBER ROOM

To combat winter's gray light (especially in a north-facing living room), set up a garden vignette with what Christopher Fox calls "uplifting elements." Fox, former creative director of the Uproar Home stores in New York and Westport, CT, starts with a small garden bistro table and one or two wire garden or ice-cream-parlor chairs. (Find these at garden or home furnishings stores and in catalogs.) Stand a topiary and another small potted plant on the table. Set a tiny indoor fountain (a "burbler," says Fox) nearby. Then stop, lest it seem contrived. You'll be reminded of the garden every time you pass by.

EDIT LIKE A PRO

What if you've pulled all the furniture together and the living room still isn't right? Try the following advice, often proffered by designers: Carry the sofa, chairs, tables, artwork,

rugs, and accessories out of the room. Now haul back only the pieces you really love. Major pieces may drift back to their former spots; that's okay. Ultimately, 50 percent of your belongings might not make it back. Chances are you simply had too much in the room, and lost sight of the things that mattered most.

SHARE YOUR GOOD FORTUNE

Redecorating means editing down, and editing means castoffs: unloved furnishings that no longer have a place in your home. They can, however, enrich another person's life. Offer donations to a local charity's thrift shop, or call a redistribution center—like those listed below—which will get your old furniture directly to someone who needs it.

San Francisco, CA: Philanthropy by Design (415) 552-1772.

Atlanta, GA: Metro Atlanta Furniture Bank (404) 355-8530.

Boston, MA: Massachusetts Coalition for the Homeless Donations Assistance Program (617) 737-3430.

Baltimore, MD: The Loading Dock (410) 728-3625.

Brooklyn, NY: Furnish a Future (718) 875-5353.

New York, NY: Materials for the Arts, New York City Department of Cultural Affairs (212) 255-5924.

Providence, RI: The Furniture Bank of Rhode Island (401) 831-5511.

Seattle, WA: The Share House Project (206) 525-1213.

Living Room Furniture in Supporting Roles

CHAPTER 5

Telling
Details and
Elegant
Display

*B*uying a sofa implies a long-term relationship, but buying a candlestick—or a mirrored switchplate, or six white McCoy vases from a flea market—is your chance to have a fling. A good, easy, sensual fling. Because details (better known as accessories) are small enough that they almost have to be quirky, or at least highly personal.

This is no time to think about propriety. Yes, there are some marvelously helpful guidelines for hanging pictures in groups or arranging things on mantels. But no law states that your mantel must be crowned by a mirror, your sofa crowned by a picture, or your candlesticks purchased in pairs.

As New York designer Craig Raywood puts it, "If you get too caught up in what's right and what's wrong, you can really miss what's beautiful."

Because accessories have a way of multiplying behind one's back, try the editing technique many designers use: Cart the lamps, pictures, and everything decorative into the hall. Now restore only what is beautiful and essential. When every object in the room has space to breathe and is something you really love, stop—and put the rest in storage.

Finally, though telling details can run small, never under-estimate the importance, or the placement, of the perfect mirror—or pillow, or vase, or picture light. They lend your living room a polished look, and can be the most expressive things you own.

A WILD BEAUTY

Animal prints appear in nearly every room that Craig Raywood designs; he finds them both exotic and natural. Any high-quality velvet or cotton fabric will do, but keep it small: a cush-ion or two, or upholstery for a footstool. Rest assured that zebra stripes and leopard spots marry easily with other classic patterns, including Oriental carpets, needlepoint rugs, and English chintz. "Animal prints have elegance," says Raywood, "and elegance, to me, has neutrality."

THE SCULPTURAL ORCHID

Treat your living room to a potted orchid. It may cost $25 to $60, but the bloom lasts four to eight weeks. Amortized, an orchid costs less than a weekly purchase of cut flowers, and its elegance carries clear across the room. "Orchids have an incredible beauty and an extravagance, but also a strong simplicity," says Raywood. Don't let the container compete with the blossom, he adds: an old terra-cotta pot will suffice.

ALLUDE TO ROYALTY

Even a relaxed living room can hint at grandeur if you work in some regal motifs. Lions, for instance, are symbolic of kings; so are bees, Napoleon's motif; the fleur-de-lis; the three Prince of Wales feathers; and the sunburst bearing a face (representing Apollo and used by French royalty). Since you aren't adorning Versailles, keep it subtle: instead of lion wallpaper, make lion-patterned pillows for the sofa. Use a Napoleonic bee fabric on side chairs, not the biggest armchair. Consider stenciling a border of fleurs-de-lis under the crown molding, rather than over the whole wall.

PLAY LIGHT AGAINST SHADOW

A table lamp, through the top of its shade, is a natural uplight. Don't let this dramatic effect go to waste: if you have a three-dimensional object to display, says New York designer Marshall Watson, hang it above the lamp. Watson has done this successfully with African masks and a paper sculpture of a horse's head. Architectural fragments would also work, as would a cast-plaster frieze. (For an old frieze, try architectural salvage yards; for reproductions, try museum shops or the Ballard and Design Toscano catalogs in Chapter 6.)

THE CONFIDENT COLLECTION

To satisfy that demanding blank spot over the sofa, many people hang a framed museum poster. For a richer and more imaginative look, collect inexpensive framed prints or watercolors from a flea market, and hang a large grouping over the sofa instead. It has more mass, collectively, than any single picture; and because the prints and frames will show their age, the pieces may even look valuable. Many designers, like Kate Stamps of the Los Angeles firm Stamps & Stamps, run the pictures straight up to the crown molding, which makes the ceiling look higher.

The ideal grouping is as wide as the sofa. It can extend over the side tables, but no farther.

Tip: Create the arrangement on the floor first.
Save the strongest pictures for the corners,
the largest for an area near the center of the group.

MIND OVER MIRROR

It's a common decorating quagmire: you move into a home whose previous owner, back in the 1970s, mirrored an entire wall. How do you make the living room less—well, glitzy? This solution comes from New York designers Scott Salvator and Michael Zabriskie:

From flea markets, gather a collection of framed prints, watercolors, or drawings. Buy sticky-backed hook-and-loop tape (better known as Velcro) in black, from a fabric or hardware store. To hang each print, stick one side of the tape all the way around the back of the picture frame, make a rectangle of equal size on the mirror where you want it to hang, and press. Create a neat, geometrical arrangement on the mirror. It will turn a highly contemporary look into something rich and traditional, and creates a focal point—saving your guests the awkwardness of studying their own reflections.

Tip: Expect to spend a number of hours measuring and rearranging before you affix the Velcro.
To simplify matters,
buy a Dry-Erase marker and eraser,
and draw the arrangement on the mirror.

KINDLE A LOW GLOW

At dusk, light a lantern—a candle in its own house of pierced metal or metal and glass. With its tiny flicker of fire, a lantern evokes a peaceful evening outdoors. Stand it on your coffee table, mantel, or wall bracket, or let it hang low from the ceiling. Countless home-design stores, from the Pottery Barn to floral-design shops, have caught on to the lantern's charm; try also Lehman's Non-Electric Catalog (see Chapter 6).

POUR ON THE LIGHT

Halogen wall sconces are fabulous sources of ambient, or general, lighting: they are discreet, sleek, and controlled by dimmers, which gives you tremendous influence over the mood of the room. A sconce should be just above eye-level, so the tallest person in the room won't be struck by glare; it should also be closed at the bottom so you can sit beneath it without being blinded.

An electrician must wire the sconce into the wall. That's easy with Sheetrock because of the plenum—the empty space behind the wallboard. But with plaster walls, there's dust involved, plus re-plastering and repainting. If you plan to live in your home for a long time, sconces are definitely worth the effort.

EVOCATIVE SALVAGE

Buy a slice of antique wrought-iron fencing, or a beautiful old gate, from an architectural salvage yard. (Nearly every city has one.) Hang it over the sofa or hearth in lieu of the usual picture or mirror.

Tip: Buy brackets at the hardware store that will let you mount the gate an inch away from the wall, advises Brooklyn designer Corey Nicholas, and the lacy ironwork will cast exquisite shadows. (Ask a carpenter to screw the brackets into the studs behind the wall.)

A BREATHTAKING CHANDELIER

Does your living room entertaining take place largely after dark? Consider a candlelit chandelier over the coffee table. "When you light the candles," says Christopher Fox, a Brooklyn designer, "there's a wonderful hush."

Find an inexpensive flea-market chandelier, preferably crystal, that holds standard (not miniature) bulbs, instructs Fox. Clip off any visible wiring. Have a *professional* carpenter or contractor install a ceiling hook that will hold the chandelier's weight. (If it crashes down when lit, it's a fire hazard.) Be prepared to relocate the coffee table so the hook can be bolted into a ceiling beam, and hang the chandelier low enough so you can easily reach the candles.

> ***Fox's anti-drip tip:*** *Burn only beeswax candles*
> *(secure in place with soft wax chips),*
> *and avoid drafts from windows or ceiling fans.*

SATISFY AN EMPTY MANTEL

If you don't own a sufficiently statuesque picture or mirror to crown the space over your mantel, have a carpenter outline that space in simple molding, as if constructing an empty picture

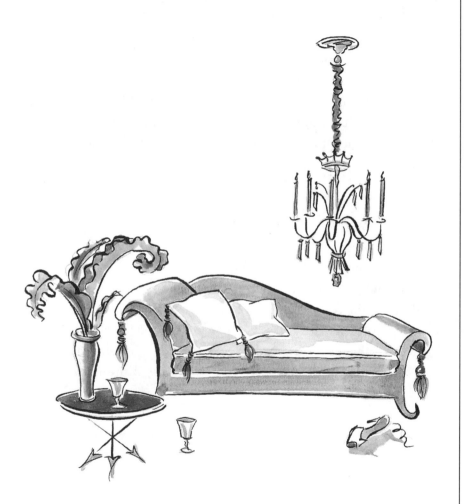

frame. (Be sure to leave a few inches of wall space all around the outside of the molding.) Now you can fill the frame with a grouping of smaller pictures or mirrors. With the molding, the group will have all the stature it needs.

Even simpler: Stand one smaller picture or mirror on the mantel and let it lean into the frame of molding, as a design editor did with much success—using nothing more than a black-and-white photograph—for the cover of *House Beautiful* magazine.

THE ARCHITECTURAL MIRROR

Here is designer Marshall Watson's mirror-over-the-mantel idea: Have a mirror supplier install a single piece of mirror to cover the entire chimney breast, the wall above the mantel. Then frame it with stock molding from the lumberyard. "Mirrors need some kind of boundary," explains Watson. Consult with a carpenter first about the dimensions of the molding and mirror.

Tip: Though framed mirrors look better with a beveled edge, wall mirror is considered an architectural usage: no bevel required.

SOLICIT THE STARS

Stand a telescope by the living room window. Not only will it draw visitors together at the window, but you may also relish using the telescope at night when you're alone.

THE TELEPHONE, AT YOUR SERVICE

Ten to one your living room has no phone. But why not? Every incoming call forces you to leap up from that comfortable chaise, or from your writing desk, and race to the bedroom or kitchen. An extension in the living room lets you bask uninterrupted. Turn off the ringer; it's intrusive and you'll hear it from other rooms anyway.

Tip: With a slim cordless phone, tangled cords won't become part of the decor. Buy it in black, a neutral color for technology.

Telling Details and Elegant Display

97

A GALLERY OF IMAGES

A photography gallery looks impressive in the living room when it's either artistic or journalistic. "Serious" photos cost hundreds or thousands of dollars, but you can also buy superb images cheaply from the pages of *The New York Times*. Collect by mood or theme: sports portraits, the urban landscape, children, whatever moves you. An 8×10 color glossy costs about $50 unframed. (The paper offers black-and-white prints, too, but they're largely made from color film, and something may be lost in translation.) Call (212) 556-1617 to request an order form.

Tip: Honor pictures with oversize mats—
a good 4 or 5 inches wide on each side—
to increase their importance.

A GALLERY OF IMAGES II

High-quality black-and-white photography can also be purchased over the Internet from companies that specialize in fine-art images at reasonable prices.

- More than 500 prints, including images by WPA photographer Dorothea Lange, are stocked by Corbis Store Fine Art & Photography. A 16×20 matte print can cost as little as $32 unframed; visit the website at www.corbistore.com.

- Fine-art photography from the 1930s and 1940s, including images by Ansel Adams, Walker Evans, and Gordon Parks, can be seen at Timeless Traveler's website: www.timelesstraveler.com. A slim catalog is available; call (888) 321-2100.

THE LITERARY HEARTH

Your fireplace may be empty because it doesn't work, or simply because of the season—either way, when unused, it's a gaping hole. Clean it well and fill with two side-by-side stacks of books. Hardcovers only, please. No matched sets. And yes, people will look, so have an honest mix of the erudite and the frivolous.

Tip: This works only if you have shelves of books elsewhere; the trick is to make it look like you stacked your extra books here, not your only books.

CULTIVATE THE SOUND OF WATER

Some designers, like Clodagh in New York, conjure serenity with the addition of an indoor fountain. The sound is exquisite, and well worth the price (roughly $200 to $300). Buy the simplest fountain possible, avoiding gimmicks, and make sure you can keep the cord out of sight. Try catalogs (Gump's, Smith & Hawken, Gardeners Eden; see Chapter 6) and garden stores.

Tip: Some shops and catalogs sell small stones that are incised with inspirational words: create, remember, joy. *Consider adding one small inspirational stone to the others in your fountain. (Two is overkill.)*

CULTIVATE A GREEN MANTEL

Most of us reflexively put flowers on coffee tables and side tables. But Bunny Williams, a top New York designer, sited eleven tall vases along a mantel at the Kips Bay Boys and Girls Club Decorator Show House. Tall flowers sprouted from about five of the vases, creating an almost architectural screen of greenery above the fireplace.

What made it work? Here's what you would have noticed in the arrangement:

- Narrow-necked vases only. (Wide-mouth vases would let the flowers lean too much, destroying the structural effect she wanted.)

- Vases of related shapes and colors (though of varying heights). These were largely pale green or white, all solid in color, and devoid of pattern.

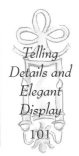

- Very tall flowers, and imposing greens—big leaves, not lacy ferns.

RELAX YOUR FLORAL DESIGN

Let flowers engage your senses in the living room, even when company's not coming. Keep them loose and informal: if you buy roses, mix them with gerbera daisies or hydrangea; if you buy tulips, place them in a vase that encourages them to lean and bend, not stand up soldier-straight.

Cut flowers several inches shorter than you're initially inclined, keeping taller blossoms toward the center of the vase. Most people leave stems too long, as if the florist had already determined the "right" height for the flower.

MAKE CANDLES A RITUAL

Burn scented candles in the living room, if you're there to keep an eye on them. Try votive candles or tea lights (which are shorter) in plain glass containers or sherry glasses so you can watch the flame—a soothing experience. Set candles near other beautiful objects: small framed photos, a vase of flowers, inlaid wooden boxes, or a piece of sculpture, so they become part of a visually pleasing composition.

Tip: All candles need watching, but votives are safest —
less likely to tip over than tapers.

LIBERATE TABLE SPACE

There's a growing trend among designers to place floor lamps, not table lamps, next to sofas or chairs. This leaves the side table free for books, flowers, and a coffee cup. Make sure light from the lamp falls on the table as well as on the sofa or chair.

Tip: If you are right-handed, the light should shine
over your left shoulder,
to avoid shadows on the page.
If you are left-handed, the reverse holds true.

THE ECCENTRIC LAMP

Living room lamps in matched pairs may look traditional, but they send an unfortunate message—that you feel safe only when you play by the rules. Have you noticed in magazines that many designers place three or four unrelated lamps in a living room? (Often they're flea-market finds, married to new shades.)

For harmony, relate the shades to each other. White silk is a classic (try an interesting shape, like a pagoda). Consider also:

- Translucent paper shades, which look like mottled alabaster when the light is on. Have a salesperson hold samples up to the bare lighted bulb in your lamp while you step back and compare variations in color. Make sure you like the paper color when the light is off, too.

- Brown kraft paper shades, which have an honest, familiar look and an amber glow. These were spotted in designer Eve Robinson's room at the Kips Bay show house, mixed in with some very expensive furnishings.

DIAL DOWN THE LIGHT

To make your living room more romantic, increase the wattage of the light bulbs to 100 or 150. (It's essential that your lamps are labeled to accept this wattage; if not, they'll need rewiring, which may cost about $30.) Then install dimmer switches and dial the brightness down. You'll get a golden-yellow light that encourages intimate conversations.

Why not just start with less wattage? Because, as lighting designer Ann Kale explains, a 100-watt bulb dimmed to 60 watts casts a yellower light—more like candlelight—than a plain 60-watt bulb.

A NINETEENTH-CENTURY DISPLAY

If your living room is blessed with picture moldings (which run about a foot below the ceiling), try using them as they were

originally intended. Buy brass gallery rods, suspend them from the moldings, and hang your framed artwork from the rods. The look is traditional, gracious, and rich, even though the rods are not all that expensive. Also, you won't pepper the walls with nail holes, as the rods are easy to adjust and move.

A single rod costs less than $30, though you will need enough for an entire room. (Pictures hung from nails look oddly weightless if their neighbors hang from rods.) To order, contact your local framer or J. Pocker & Son, 135 East 63rd Street, New York, NY 10021; tel. (212) 838-5488; fax (212) 752-2172.

Tip: Ask for rods with an "ogee" (round) bend at the top; they will fit most picture moldings.

THE VOLUPTUOUS PILLOW

Austin designer Hortensia Vitali gets the most luxurious throw pillows from flea markets—in the form of old cashmere coats, which she takes to her upholsterer for transformation. She also snaps up old fur muffs, like the leopard muff she found at a garage sale, took apart, and turned into a pair of velvet-backed pillows. (Don't try this at home; only upholsterers have the proper equipment to sew fur.)

THE CLASSICALLY ELEGANT PILLOW

Vitali's favorite pillow shape follows the golden mean, an ancient rule of proportion that governed the architecture of the Parthenon and Palladian villas.

Whip out the calculator: the length of the pillow should be 1.6 times its height, creating a golden rectangle. (A 12-inch-long pillow would thus be 7½ inches high; an 18-inch-long pillow, 11¼ inches high.)

THE CLASSICALLY ELEGANT PILLOW II

New York designer Benjamin Noriega-Ortiz comes close to the golden rectangle with this shortcut: He makes pillows twice as long as they are high. He also makes them with restraint—just a handful, scattered around the room, suffices. If you have to compete with the pillows for space on your sofa, he says, edit them down.

CONQUER THE CATHEDRAL CEILING

Small objects can look lost under a cathedral ceiling. Scale everything up, advises Chicago designer Richar. If you have no huge paintings, hang textiles from rods high on the wall. At

eye-level, group small pictures into larger assemblages. Have at least one overscaled piece of furniture in the room. Under a lofty ceiling, says Richar, "size creates total drama."

Tip: Camouflage the cord. A picture light is the crowning glory on a piece of art you love—but designers can't sleep when the cords from picture lights trail down the wall. (They are supposed to be wired in.) If you truly have no choice, says New York designer Marshall Watson, paint the cord the color of the wall and make sure it drops neat and straight so it will make itself less visible.

CHAPTER 6

The Best Mail-Order Resources for Living Rooms

I've tried to include the quirky as well as the classic, particularly for readers who don't live near major shopping districts. Catalog prices can change, so they're not listed here—but many of these catalogs are free.

Anthropologie
One Margaret Way
Ridgely, MD 21685
(800) 309-2500
www.anthropologie.com
   A marvelously eccentric assortment of lighting, drapery, cabinetry, voluptuous leather and slipcovered seating, hanging glass lanterns, and elegant but understated throw pillows. Even if you live near an Anthropologie store, the catalog is worth perusing.

Ballard Designs
1670 DeFoor Avenue N.W.
Atlanta, GA 30318
(800) 367-2775

The catalog you'd choose for a desert island. Upholstered furniture (a few pieces with down-blend filling), architectural ornaments, throw pillows, lighting of every description, coffee tables, mirrors overscaled to fit over a hearth, round sofa tables and the skirts with which to drape them, even the topiary to set upon them. Note the étagères, tall and short, for books, plants, even office equipment.

The Bright Spot
33 Chestnut Street
Westmont, IL 60559
Tel. (800) 736-0126
Fax (800) 736-1329

Copies and adaptations of handsome Arts and Crafts lighting . . . handsome, though at a price. A brass sconce inspired by Frank Lloyd Wright approaches $400. Spider, a Tiffany design, costs nearly $700, though it lives up to its description: "Darkened, it is a deliciously sinister masterpiece of dark brooding power."

Calico Corners
203 Gale Lane
Kennett Square, PA 19348
(800) 213-6366

Leopard-print velvet, cotton chenille, paisley tapestry—it's amazing how easily fabrics can be purchased by mail, especially when you can borrow a yard before deciding. Traditionally styled sofas and chair-plus-ottoman marriages are offered, too; they arrive upholstered in your choice of fabric.

Country Curtains
At the Red Lion Inn
Stockbridge, MA 01262
(800) 456-0321

Many of these curtains cross the line of cuteness, but the curtain *jewelry* is a great idea.

Craftsman Homes Connection
2525 East 29th Street, Suite 10B-343
Spokane, WA 99223
Tel. (509) 535-5098
www.crafthome.com

All of the furnishings and accessories here are inspired by the Arts and Crafts style. Among them: andirons, CD storage racks, coasters, small tables, Mission-style mirrors, rugs, lighting, pottery, and clocks. Don't miss the extensive and user-friendly website.

Crate & Barrel
P.O. Box 3200
Naperville, IL 60566
(800) 323-5461
 Coffee tables, chairs, pillows, rugs, lighting, and shelving units, all in contemporary, pared-down styles.

Design Toscano
1645 Greenleaf Avenue
Elk Grove Village, IL 60007
(800) 525-0733
 Cast copies of sculptures, architectural fragments, and ornamental friezes to hang over the hearth.

Elements
P.O. Box 6105
Rapid City, SD 57709
(800) 778-5555
www.elementscatalogue.com
 From Spiegel, a sophisticated and pared-down selection of rugs, tables, chairs, screens, little tables, pillows, and accessories.

Exposures Homes
P.O. Box 3615
Oshkosh, WI 54903
(800) 699-6993
 Upholstered furniture, side and coffee tables, and a stylish but simple assortment of frames, vases, candles, lighting, and other accessories.

Gardeners Eden
17 Riverside Street
Nashua, NH 03062
(800) 822-9600
 Amid the flowers and wreathes, some rustic indoor furnishings: benches, chests, cabinets, lithe metal chairs, indoor fountains.

Garnet Hill
231 Main Street
Franconia, NH 03580
(800) 622-6216
    Yes, this is largely a bedroom catalog. But the luxurious throws, the occasional chaise, the intriguing rugs, the living room tables, and a lamp here and there make it worth examining.

Gump's By Mail
P.O. Box 489
New Oxford, PA 17350
(800) 284-8677
www.gumpsbymail.com
    Furnishings and accessories with an exotic note, including faux bamboo folding tables; little altar and tea tables that can serve as a second tier for display on your coffee table. Also: a few terrific indoor fountains.

Hold Everything
P.O. Box 7807
San Francisco, CA 94120
(800) 421-2264
    Shelving, self-inflating mattresses (less expensive than a pull-out sofa), handsome boxes to corral magazines and papers, lighting.

IKEA
8352 Honeygo Boulevard
Baltimore, MD 21236
(800) 434-IKEA
www.ikea.com
    Armchairs, sofas, artwork, storage units, curtains, rugs, lighting, tables—just be selective, as a roomful of blond wood may resemble an Ikea ad. Mix Ikea's staples with pricier items, including antiques, and they'll blend right in.

Illuminations
1995 South McDowell Boulevard
Petaluma, CA 94954
(800) CANDLES
    Tapers, pillar candles, votives, and the beautiful Rituals Candles formulated to enhance such "essential qualities" as thankfulness, happiness, love, courage, and passion.

J. Jill Homewear
P.O. Box 2006, 100 Birch Pond Drive
Tilton, NH 03276
(800) 642-9989

From the clothing company J. Jill comes furniture with natural tones and textures: jute rugs, leather and rattan tables, leather chairs, candles—a small collection, but worth keeping an eye on.

Legacy
514 North Third Street
Minneapolis, MN 55401
(800) 328-2711

Every three months Legacy comes out with another themed catalog—lodge style, for example, or Swedish style. Depending on the genre, watch for armchairs, settees, andirons, throw pillows, rugs, even an exquisite lace hammock.

Lehman's Non-Electric Catalog
One Lehman Circle, P.O. Box 41
Kidron, OH 44636
(330) 857-5757
www.lehmans.com

Sells the most gorgeous sconce anywhere: a Victorian cast-metal bracket (called a "bracket lamp") that can hold pillar candles or a miniature gas lamp, sold separately. A silvery glass reflector can be added to magnify the light.

Levenger
420 S. Congress Avenue
Delray Beach, FL 33445
(800) 544-0880

Writing desks, shelving, some unusual and highly functional lamps, end tables with shelves for books and magazines.

Martha By Mail
P.O. Box 60060
Tampa, FL 33660
(800) 950-7130
www.marthastewart.com

Though Martha's catalog tends to focus on kitchens and bedrooms, her accessories can add grace notes anywhere: trays, throw pillows, French flower buckets, candles in her trademark pale pastels.

The Best Mail-Order Resources for Living Rooms

113

Mig and Tig Furniture
549 North Wells
Chicago, IL 60610
(312) 644-8277
   Sofas, deep and velvet-covered; also coffee tables of iron and wood, wall plaques, lighting, and such accessories as a gargoyle-shaped plant stand.

Museum of Modern Art
Mail Order Department
11 West 53rd Street
New York, NY 10019
(800) 447-6662
   A narrow but well-edited selection of modern classics, like a storage unit by Charles and Ray Eames, Noguchi lamps, Alvar Aalto chairs and stools, a sleek folding table, a set of blue thermoplastic nesting tables . . . an indispensable catalog.

The Natural Choice
Eco Design Company
1365 Rufina Circle
Santa Fe, NM 87505
(800) 621-2591
   The paints, stains, thinners, milk paint, and glazes in this catalog are made with naturally derived materials, from citrus and seed oils to beeswaxes and earth pigments. The paint comes in white; you choose pigments from a color chart and add them yourself.

Outwater Plastics Industries
4 Passaic Street, P.O. Drawer 403
Wood-Ridge, NJ 07075
(888) OUTWATER
www.outwater.com
   Designer Kim DePole's favorite—a 929-page, black-and-white catalog of industrial products, like the racks and stands used for store displays. (Try them for family photos and potted plants.) Also: mirrored panels, Orac Decor moldings, and racks for CDs with which you can panel an entire wall, if you want. A great catalog if you bring your own creativity to it.

Pottery Barn
P.O. Box 7044
San Francisco, CA 94120
(800) 922-5507

Designers often mix Pottery Barn items in with pedigreed pieces. Look for vintage-style fans, throw pillows, wall vases, tables, rugs, and window treatments, not to mention sofas and chairs.

Restoration Hardware
104 Challenger Drive
Portland, TN 37148
(800) 762-1005
   Evocative furnishings, from a slipcovered rocker to a trio of nesting tables inspired by clean, 1940s designs. Also: lighting, fireplace accessories, sofas and chairs, and Silver Sage paint—the exact shade of green used in the firm's stores. (Call for a swatch.)

Room
151 West 30th Street, Suite 705
New York, NY 10001
(888) 420-ROOM
   Living room sofas, chairs, tables, wine racks, lighting, screens and cushions, and, at some point, a collection of custom photography. Most pieces can be ordered with custom finishes and fabrics, and other custom services can be requested. Room looks like a sleek design magazine, except that everything on its pages is for sale.

Shaker Workshops
P.O. Box 8001
Ashburnham, MA 01430
(800) 840-9121
www.shakerworkshops.com
   This catalog is full of patterned accessories that would have appalled Mother Ann Lee, but the furniture—chairs, tables, pegboard, candlestands, shelving, even a coffee table shaped like a Shaker oval box—retains the trademark crisp lines.

Smith & Hawken Home & Clothing
2 Arbor Lane, Box 6900
Florence, KY 41022
(800) 776-3336
www.smith-hawken.com
   Coffee tables, lamps, inviting armchairs of rattan and water hyacinth, candles, screens, and ceramics. The selection isn't vast, but it's superbly edited.

The Best Mail-Order Resources for Living Rooms

Smith+Noble Windoware
·P.O. Box 1838
Corona, CA 91718
(800) 248-8888

Clean-lined and classic window treatments at truly discount prices, though you must supply your own measurements (with expert guidance from the catalog). The bamboo shades, fabric blinds, and wooden blinds are particularly suited to living rooms.

Spiegel
P.O. Box 182555
Columbus, OH 43218
(800) 345-4500

Costly, at $10, for a catalog, but worth it for the rugs, window treatments, upholstered furnshings, lighting, tables, throw pillows, and fireplace furnishings.

Whispering Pines: Things for the Cabin
43 Ruane Street
Fairfield, CT 06430
(800) 836-4662

Rustic accessories for the Adirondack cabin of your dreams: cast-iron lanterns that hold votive candles, small side tables made from branches, lamps, rugs, and unusual throw pillows.